appetising

hors d'oeuvres

TRIDENT PRESS
INTERNATIONAL

Published by:
TRIDENT PRESS INTERNATIONAL
801, 12th Avenue South
Suite 302
Naples, Fl 34102 USA
Copyright (c)Trident Press International 2001
Email: tridentpress@worldnet.att.net
Website: www.trident-international.com

acknowledgements

Appetising Hors d'oeuvres
Compiled by: R&R Publications Marketing P/L
Creative Director: Paul Sims
Production Manager: Anthony Carroll
Food Photography: Warren Webb,
Food Stylists: Stephane Souvlis, Janet Lodge,
Di Kirby,
Recipe Development: Ellen Argyriou,
Sheryle Eastwood, Kim Freedman,
Lucy Kelly, Donna Hay,
Proof Reader: Andrea Hazell-tarttelin

Includes Index
ISBN 1 582791 16 3
EAN 9 781582 791 16 6

First Edition Printed February 2001
Computer Typeset in Humanist 521
& Times New Roman

Printed by Toppan, Hong Kong
Film Scanning by DPI, Sydney Australia

contents

introduction

introduction

Fabulous hors d'oevres

The modern trend appears to be moving to more casual entertaining. What better way to entertain family and friends than by providing easy-to-eat food. Hors d'oeuvres allows you to prepare a variety of foods to suit just about everyone's taste.

We all remember a special dip or spread from our childhood...and how many times have you been moved to seek the recipe of a superb-tasting morsel from your hosts?

The recipes that follow have been specially created to provide you with many new ideas which we are sure will quickly become part of your entertainment repertoire and long-term family favourites.

Recipes that follow will smooth the way to cooking for informal gatherings, brunches, lunches, cocktail parties, patio parties and buffets. These stylish, economical recipes have been created for the busy cook and all recipes contain ingredients easily found on your supermarket shelves.

Many recipes can be prepared well ahead of time thereby allowing you, the cook, time enough to enjoy the company of your guests.

How to Give a Successful Party

How often have you thought about giving a party and been put off by the idea of the food preparation involved? Serving drinks is one thing, catering for a crowd is another.

This book has all the answers. Here, for the first time, is a complete selection of delectable hors d'oeuvres to entertain your guests, no matter what the occasion — formal or informal, outdoors or indoors, summer or winter.

The recipes are simple to make, use attractive ingredients, and are designed to give you maximum time enjoying the company of your guests. Most can be prepared beforehand, with little or no last-minute time to spend.

The key word is simplicity. Every single recipe in this book is meant to be eaten with fingers only — no forks or knives please! The only other things you as party-giver have to provide are: the occasion, good cheer and plenty of napkins!

As goes for mixing and matching between the sections in this book, let your imagination go and have fun!

easy antipasto

Easy antipasto platter for six
An antipasto platter is fun as a starter to an Italian meal, or to serve when friends drop by.

- **Vegetable Toss**
- **Crostini**
- **Prosciutto with Melon**
- **Creamy Tuna Spread**
- **Salami Platter**
- **Marinated Olives**
- **Eggplant (aubergine) with Dipping Sauce**

Vegetable Toss
Make this dish several hours ahead of time to allow the flavours to develop.

2 tablespoons olive oil
4 zucchini (courgettes), sliced lengthways
1 large head broccoli, cut into florets
2 carrots, peeled
Dressing
2 small red chillies, finely chopped
1 tablespoon each fresh mint and fresh oregano, finely chopped
1/2 cup/125ml/4 1/2fl oz light olive oil
2 tablespoons red wine vinegar
2 tablespoons lemon juice
freshly ground black pepper

1 *Heat oil in a skillet and cook zucchini (courgette) slices until golden on each side. Drain on paper towels and set aside.*
2 *Boil, steam or microwave broccoli until tender. Refresh under cold water. Drain and set aside.*
3 *Slice carrots into long thin strips, using a vegetable peeler. Boil, steam or microwave until just tender. Refresh under cold water. Drain and set aside.*
4 *To make dressing: place chillies, mint, oregano, oil, vinegar and lemon juice in a screwtop jar. Season to taste with pepper. Shake well to combine. Place vegetables in a serving bowl and toss through dressing. Cover and refrigerate until required.*
Serves 6

Crostini
This recipe can be made using any of your favourite breads.

1 loaf Italian bread, cut into 1cm/1/2in slices
1/3 cup/90g/3oz butter, melted

1 *Lightly brush both sides of bread slices with butter and place on a cookie sheet.*
2 *Bake at 180°C/350°F for 12 minutes, or until golden and crunchy.*
Serves 6

Prosciutto with Melon

1 cantaloupe (rockmelon) or honeydew melon, halved, seeded and peeled
18 slices prosciutto ham

1 *Cut melon into 18 long thin wedges, wrap a slice of prosciutto around each wedge of melon and secure with a wooden pick. Arrange on platter and chill before serving.*
Makes 18

Creamy Tuna Spread
This spread is great served with Crostini or fresh crusty bread.

185g/6oz canned tuna, drained
1/2 cup/125g/4 1/2oz cream cheese
1/2 cup/125g/4 1/2oz mayonnaise
2 tablespoons lemon juice
1/2 cup/125g/4 1/2oz butter, melted
1 teaspoon snipped fresh chives
1 teaspoon chopped fresh thyme

1 *Place tuna, cream cheese, mayonnaise and lemon juice in a food processor or blender and process until smooth. With machine running, add butter, chives and thyme. Transfer mixture to a serving dish and refrigerate for 1 hour or until firm.*
Serves 6

Salami Selection

125g/4½oz each of any 2 types of sliced Italian salami (such as: alesandre, felino, cotto, felinetti, calabrese, Napoli, Milano and Genoa)
125g/4½oz each of any 2 types of sliced Italian hams or sausages (such as: pastrami, pancetta, mortadella and pepperoni)

1 *Cut or fold salami, hams and sausages to make your platter look appealing.*
    Serves 6

Marinated Olives

These olives will keep for up to four months in the refrigerator.
375g/12oz black olives, drained
Marinade
½ cup/125ml/4½fl oz light olive oil
¼ cup/60ml/2fl oz balsamic vinegar
1 tablespoon fresh tarragon, chopped
2 bay leaves
2 tablespoons fresh basil, chopped
2 teaspoons freshly ground black pepper

1 *Place olives in a large sterilised jar. Mix together oil, vinegar, tarragon, bay leaves, basil and black pepper. Pour over olives to cover. Seal jar and store in refrigerator.*
    Makes a 500ml/1 pint jar

Eggplant (aubergine) with Dipping Sauce

1 eggplant (aubergine), cut in half lengthwise, then into 5mm/¼in slices
salt
¾ cup/185g/6½oz cornflour (cornstarch)
vegetable oil for cooking
Dipping sauce
1 red capsicum (pepper), seeded, coarsely chopped
⅓ cup/100ml/3½fl oz light cream

¼ cup/60g/2oz butter, chopped

¼ teaspoon chilli powder
freshly ground black pepper
Batter
1 cup/125g/4½oz flour
1 teaspoon baking powder
¾ cup/200ml/7fl oz milk
2 eggs, lightly beaten

1 *Sprinkle eggplant (aubergine) slices with salt and set aside for 30 minutes.*
2 *To make sauce: place red capsicum (pepper) and cream in a food processor or blender and process until smooth. Transfer to a small saucepan and cook over low heat for 5 minutes. Remove from heat and whisk in butter. Season to taste with chilli powder and black pepper. Set aside; keep warm.*
3 *To make batter: Sift flour and baking powder into a small bowl, make a well in the centre and gradually stir in milk and eggs. Mix to form a smooth paste. Set aside.*
4 *Rinse eggplant (aubergine) well under cold running water. Drain and pat dry on paper towels. Toss eggplant in cornflour (cornstarch) and shake to remove excess.*
5 *Heat oil in a skillet. Dip eggplant (aubergine) slices in batter and cook a few at a time until golden brown. Drain on paper towels. Serve eggplant (aubergine) with warm sauce.*
    Serves 6

mushroom melts

cheese snacks

All foods have a greater appeal

if they are attractively presented, and cheese is no exception. Invest in a cheese board, or bring out a handsome platter and surround your cheese (a choice of varieties, or just your favourite cheddar) with cracker biscuits, celery, radishes, or a lovely wreath of fresh fruit. Cheese and fruit are regarded as the perfect dessert combination by many European gourmets – and for health and sheer good eating we might follow their example.

cheese

There are hundreds of distinct varieties of cheese, but no matter how different the finished product, they all started out the same way.

Firm Cheeses

Cheddar cheese is by far the most popular of cheeses. It ranges from mild to full-flavoured; nothing can challenge it for versatility. Equally delicious in salads, savouries, sandwiches, it is a tasty addition to soups and meat dishes, and as a high energy snack with fruit, when served with crackers.

Other varieties of cheeses are:

Swiss (or Gruyère or Emmenthale) – Used for salads, sandwiches, fondue and popular as a dessert cheese.

Edam – A mild close-textured cheese, is relished as a dessert cheese served with fruit or a selection of cracker biscuits.

Gouda (rhyming with "chowder") – Greatly resembles Edam in taste and style.

Provolone – A smooth hard cheese, with a robust smoky, sometimes salty taste. Excellent for hors d'oeuvres, snacks and hearty cheese dishes. A good grating cheese, with character, everyone should make a point of at least sampling Provolone.

Soft Cheeses fall into two classes – ripened and unripened:

Soft Ripened Cheese – Many famous varieties come into this class. Some of them need careful handling on account of their delicate consistency, but they all keep well, if protected from heat and air.

Blue Vein – This cheese has many illustrious predecessors, including France's Roquefort, Italy's Gorgonzola, Denmark's Danablu and England's Stilton. Particularly good for appetisers and savoury spreads and dips, it is delicious with all crackers.

Feta – A moist, very white cheese made extensively in Greece and the Balkans, traditionally made from sheep or goat's milk. Always delicious but can be a little salty, particularly enjoyable with dark bread and olives.

Mozzarella – A famous Italian cheese, in demand for both table and cooking. Because of its fast-melting properties it is always used in authentic pizza. A mild but exceptionally pleasing flavour with a slightly resilient texture. Great for melts or grilled on toast, also delicious as a topping for meat loaves, casseroles and melted on crumbed cutlets.

Soft Unripened Cheeses

Cottage and **cream cheeses** have a variety of tastes from mild and bland as the American or sharper as the Continental style. These cheeses are best served chilled and have many delicious uses: in salads, spreads and dips, with fruit, as a filling for pancakes and omelettes and, of course, as the principle ingredient in all types of cheesecake. Italian-style **ricotta** is a similar cheese of delicate bland flavour which can be use a in the same manner as cottage and cream cheeses.

Hard Grating Cheeses

Parmesan – An almost rock-hard, dry cheese with a full and deliciously piquant flavour. Adds great flavour to soups, pasta, meat dishes, vegetables, savouries, stuffings, sauces and risottos. Keeps well and does not normally need refrigeration.

Romana – The mildest of the grating cheeses, it makes an exciting difference to many recipes.

Pecorino – The strongest and most pungent of the grating cheeses. Made from ewe's milk in Italy where it derives its name from the Italian name for sheep. In Australia it is normally made from cow's milk. Richer than Parmesan and much more robust in flavour.

apricots
with blue-cheese topping

Photograph page 11

Method:

1 *Cut apricots in half and remove seed (or drain canned apricots well on absorbent paper).*

2 *Place apricots cut side up on serving plate and spread each with a teaspoon of cheese.*

3 *If desired, apricots and cheese may be grilled for about 1 minute or until cheese begins to melt. Serve immediately.*

Makes 24

ingredients

**12 fresh apricots or
1 x 850g/28oz can apricot halves
250g/¹/₂ lb soft blue cheese**

cheese
and chive croquettes

Photograph opposite

Method:

1 *Place mozzarella cheese, 1 cup/125g/4oz flour, chives, cayenne pepper and eggs in a bowl and mix to combine. Shape mixture into balls, place on a plate lined with plastic food wrap and refrigerate for 30 minutes.*

2 *Combine cornflour (cornstarch) and remaining flour on a plate. Roll balls in flour mixture and chill for 10 minutes.*

3 *Heat oil in a saucepan (until a cube of bread dropped in browns in 50 seconds) and deep-fry croquettes, in batches, for 4-5 minutes, or until golden. Drain on absorbent kitchen paper and serve.*

Makes 24

ingredients

**500g/1 lb grated mozzarella cheese
1¹/₂ cups/185g/6oz flour
4 tablespoons snipped fresh chives
¹/₂ teaspoon cayenne pepper
2 eggs, lightly beaten
¹/₂ cup/60g/2oz cornflour (cornstarch)
vegetable oil for deep-frying**

cheese
twisties

ingredients

**2 sheets ready-rolled puff pastry
1 egg
1/2 cup/60g/2oz cheese, finely grated**

Method:

1 Brush the first sheet of pastry lightly with egg and sprinkle with cheese.
2 Brush the second sheet of pastry lightly with egg and place over the cheese.
3 Press the pastry sheets firmly together. Cut the pastry in half and then cut each half into 2cm/1in-wide strips.
4 Pick up each strip of pastry with both hands and twist before placing on a sheet of baking paper on an oven tray.
5 Bake in an oven at 230°C/450°F for 10 minutes or until golden. Serve warm.
Variation: Use 1 slice of finely chopped bacon and 1 tablespoon of finely chopped pecans to replace the cheese.

14
Makes 20

cheese
and garlic pita wedges

Method:

1 *Split pita bread in half, cut each half into 4 wedges.*
2 *Combine butter, garlic and basil, brush over cut side of bread wedges, then sprinkle with Parmesan cheese.*
3 *Place in single layer on oven trays, bake in moderate oven for 10 minutes or until crisp.*

Makes 32 wedges

ingredients

4 white pita bread
125g/4oz butter, melted
3 cloves garlic, crushed
2 tablespoons chopped fresh basil
1/3 cup/45g/1 1/2oz grated Parmesan cheese

baby squash
with capsicum (pepper) and cheese filling

Photograph opposite

Method:

1 *Cook squash in boiling water until tender, drain, cool. Scoop out top part of each squash.*
2 *Combine capsicum, cheese, egg, spring onions and cayenne pepper. Spoon into squash.*
3 *Bake in a moderate oven for 10 minutes or until heated through.*
   Makes 24

ingredients

**24 yellow baby squash
1 large capsicum (pepper), finely chopped
1/2 cup/60g/2oz tasty cheese (mature Cheddar), grated
1 egg, lightly beaten
2 spring onions (scallions), finely chopped
1/4 teaspoon cayenne pepper**

stuffed
celery sticks

Method:

1 *Place all ingredients except celery, in a food processor and process until ingredients are combined and smooth.*
2 *Fill celery sticks with cheese mixture, arrange on a serving platter with slices of carrot as garnish.*
   Makes about 25

ingredients

**6 sticks celery, cut into 2 1/2cm/1in lengths
100g/3 1/2oz blue-vein cheese, cubed
125g/4 1/2oz cream cheese, cubed
1 teaspoon brandy
freshly ground black pepper**

toasted
cheese snacks

ingredients

6 slices brown bread
2 teaspoons mild mustard
6 slices cooked chicken or chicken roll
125g/4oz Cheddar cheese, grated
3 tablespoons mayonnaise
2 spring onions, finely chopped

Method:
1 *Toast bread, then spread each slice with a little of the mustard. Top with a slice of chicken or chicken roll.*
2 *Combine cheese, mayonnaise and spring onions in a bowl; mix well. Spread cheese mixture on top of each chicken slice.*
3 *Cook under a preheated grill for about 3 minutes, or until cheese mixture bubbles. Serves at once with a salad garnish if desired.*
Serves 3-6

bubbly cheese,
ham and pineapple toasts

ingredients

250g/8oz Cheddar cheese, grated
90g/3oz lean cooked ham, chopped
2 eggs, lightly beaten
8 slices wholewheat bread
8 canned pineapple rings

Method:
1 *Combine cheese and ham in a mixing bowl. Add beaten egg and mix lightly. Set aside.*
2 *Toast bread slices on one side only under a preheated grill. Turn bread slices over and top each untoasted side with a pineapple ring. Pile cheese mixture on top, spreading it out to cover toast completely.*
3 *Return toasts to grill until topping is bubbly and golden brown. Serve at once.*
Serves 8

cheese
puffs

Method:

1. Combine cheese, breadcrumbs, egg yolks, mustard, paprika, salt and pepper. Mix well.
2. Beat egg whites until stiff. Gently fold into the cheese mixture.
3. Shape mixture into small, walnut sized, balls. Roll in extra breadcrumbs.
4. Deep fry, a few at a time, until golden brown, about 30 seconds.

Serves 4

4 cups/500g/1 lb grated tasty cheese
1 cup/90g/3oz fresh breadcrumbs
4 eggs, separated
1 teaspoon dry mustard
1 teaspoon paprika
salt and pepper
fresh breadcrumbs, extra
oil for deep frying

tuna
melts

Method:

1 *Sauté the onions in the butter till soft and golden. Add the drained tuna, salt, pepper and Tabasco. Stir to mix ingredients and to flake the tuna. Allow to cool.*
2 *Place a teaspoonful of mixture on each water cracker biscuit. Cut each cheese slice into strips. Place a few strips over tuna mixture on each biscuit.*
3 *Cut a slice of gherkin and place on top. Set under hot grill until cheese melts and the tuna mixture is covered.*

Serves 4

ingredients

1 small onion, finely chopped
2 teaspoons butter
185g/6^1/$_4$oz can tuna in oil, drained
salt and pepper
^{1}/$_4$ teaspoon Tabasco
16 water cracker biscuits
4 sandwich cheese slices
2 sweet gherkins

mushroom
melts

Method:

1 Melt butter in a small pan, add shallots, mushrooms and garlic and sauté a little. Add salt, pepper and lemon juice. Stir in flour and cook 1 minute. Allow to cool.

2 Place a teaspoonful on each water cracker biscuit. Cut each cheese slice into four squares. Place a piece over the mushroom mixture on each cracker.

3 Place under hot grill until cheese melts. Sprinkle with paprika and serve.

Serves 4

ingredients

2 teaspoons butter
2 tablespoons finely chopped shallots
150g/5¹/₂oz mushrooms, chopped
¹/₂ teaspoon crushed garlic
¹/₄ teaspoon each salt and pepper
2 teaspoons lemon juice
2 teaspoons flour
16 water cracker biscuits
4 sandwich cheese slices
paprika

prawn (shrimp) melts

Method:

1 *Reserve 16 prawns (shrimp) for garnish and chop the remainder. Mix in lemon juice, salt and pepper.*

2 *Place a teaspoonful of mixture on each cracker. Cut cheese slice into quarters. Place a piece over prawn (shrimp) mixture then garnish top with a reserved prawn (shrimp).*

3 *Place under a hot grill until cheese melts and covers the prawn (shrimp) filling; this will fix the prawn (shrimp) garnish in place.*

Serves 4

ingredients

**250g/9oz small school prawns (shrimp)
2 teaspoons lemon juice
salt and pepper
16 water cracker biscuits
4 sandwich cheese slices**

mini spinach
and cheese quiches

Method:

1 Cut pastry into 6cm/2½in rounds with a pastry cutter and press into shallow patty pans.
2 In a food processor, process the cheese, spinach, onion, egg, cream, parsley, mustard, salt and pepper until all ingredients are finely chopped and well combined.
3 Spoon 1 tablespoon of mixture into each patty pan.
4 Bake in a hot 210°C/410°F oven for 20 minutes, or until puffed and golden.
5 Remove from pans, place on platter and serve.
Variations: Crab and Ham: Substitute cheese, spinach and parsley with a 170g/6oz can crab meat, drained and 125g/4½oz sliced ham. **Cheese and Ham:** Substitute spinach leaves with 125g/4½oz sliced ham.

Makes about 24

ingredients

**3 sheets ready-rolled puff pastry
125g/4½oz tasty cheese
(mature Cheddar), cubed
2 spinach leaves, washed and torn into
large strips, with stems removed
½ small onion, peeled and halved
1 egg
3 tablespoons cream
1 tablespoon parsley sprigs,
firmly packed
1 tablespoon French mustard
salt & pepper**

crocked
cheese

Photograph opposite

ingredients

¼ cup/60g/2oz cottage cheese
¼ cup/60g/2oz ricotta cheese
½ cup/60g/2oz grated Cheddar cheese
65g/2oz butter
½ cup/30g/1oz shallots, chopped
30ml/1fl oz beer
1 teaspoon Dijon mustard
1 teaspoon paprika
¼ teaspoon salt
1-2 teaspoons poppy seeds
1 packet crackers
extra poppy seeds for garnish

Method:
1 Combine all ingredients in a food processor. Blend well. Turn the mixture into a crock or serving bowl. Sprinkle additional poppy seeds on top for garnish.
2 Refrigerate until ready to serve. Serve with an assortment of crackers.
Makes about 1 ½ cups/360g/12oz dip

sun-dried
tomato and goat's cheese pâté

ingredients

90g/3oz sun-dried tomatoes, drained and chopped
125g/4½oz goat's cheese
pinch dried thyme
2 teaspoons finely chopped parsley
1 packet cracked-pepper water crackers

Method:
1 Combine all ingredients in a food processor and purée.
2 Serve with cracked-pepper water crackers.
Makes about 1 cup/240g/8oz of pâté

honey-glazed spareribs

meat treats

To eat well in the company of friends

and family is one of life's great pleasures. In the rush and dash of workaday life, cooking for fun rather than out of necessity seems an unattainable dream. But, as you'll find in this section beautifully presented easy-to-prepare beef, lamb, pork and chicken finger food is within reach of us all, no matter how little time we have, and regardless of our level of culinary skill.

meat

Nutritive Value of Meat

Lean beef, lamb, pork and chicken are highly nutritious foods with unique features. Low in fat, yet packed full of high-quality protein and essential vitamins and minerals, lean meat is a valuable contributor to a healthy body. One of meat's prime nutritional benefits is as a supplier of the mineral iron, which is indispensable in carrying oxygen around our bodies, via the bloodstream. If you do not get enough iron you may become tired, have poor stamina and even become anaemic.

Lean beef, lamb, pork and chicken are some of the highest iron foods and this so-called "haem iron" is the most easily used by our bodies. The "haem iron" in meat also helps the body maximise the iron in poorer iron ("non-haem") foods, such as vegetables, nuts, legumes and grains.

Purchasing of Meat

Getting the best out of meat buying relies on the correct choice of cuts, the correct purchasing and storage of meat, and the correct cooking methods of the meat selected. Choosing cuts of meat suitable for each dish is nominated in the recipes that follow.

- Only buy the amount of meat which can be stored correctly in the space available.
- Before setting out to purchase a fresh supply of meat, prepare the refrigerator and freezer ready for meat storage. Make the necessary space available, wash meat trays and defrost the refrigerator and freezer if necessary, so that meat will be stored immediately on arriving home.
- Choose meat that is bright in colour, with a fresh (not dry) appearance.
- Keep meat cold whilst carrying home to prevent the growth of food-spoilage bacteria. This may be achieved by using an insulated chiller bag. For larger quantities, if transporting by car, place in a car chiller and store the meat in it as soon as purchased, particularly if departure for home is not immediate.

- If you are unsure about which cuts to buy seek advice from your butcher – trained professionals who are always willing to assist.
- If calculating the quantity of meat to buy for a meal is a problem, allow 125-150g/4¹/2-5¹/2oz of lean boneless meat per person.

Storage of Meat

In the Meat Compartment:

Remove from pre-package (plastic makes meat sweat which shortens shelf life), and arrange in stacks no more than 2-3 layers high. Make sure there is some air space between each piece of meat. Cover top of meat loosely with foil or greaseproof paper to stop surface drying.

In the Refrigerator Cabinet:

Place a stainless steel or plastic rack in a dish deep enough to catch any meat drippage. Unwrap meat and store as for "Meat Compartment", in the coldest part of the refrigerator. This is normally in the bottom of the refrigerator. If meat is to be used on the day of purchase, it can be left in its original wrapping.

Meat kept in the refrigerator for 2-3 days will be more tender than meat cooked on day of purchase.

In the Freezer:

Pack chops and steaks in 2 layers only, with freezer wrap between each layer, so that they separate easily. Pack flat in freezer bags.

Defrost meats in the refrigerator – never at room temperature or in water. Allow 2 days for a large roast, 1 day or less for smaller cuts, according to quantity. Do not remove from package when thawing. Meat may also be defrosted quickly in a microwave oven.

Do not refreeze thawed meat unless cooked first. Frozen meats should be stored at a constant temperature of -15°C/5°F.

Prolonged storage time in the freezer will result in loss of quality.

cocktail
meatballs

Photograph page 29

ingredients

Meatballs

250g/9oz minced beef

1 onion, grated

2 tablespoons dried breadcrumbs

1/2 teaspoon salt

1 egg

1 tablespoon chopped parsley

1/4 teaspoon pepper

1/4 teaspoon oregano

1 teaspoon Tabasco sauce

Filling

8 prunes, pitted and chopped

1 tablespoon pine nuts,
coarsely chopped

Method:

1 Mix mince and all ingredients for meat balls together, knead well with hands until mince becomes fine in grain. Allow to stand for 15 minutes before rolling.

2 Combine prunes and pine nuts. Wet palms of hands to prevent mince sticking, take about a tablespoon of mince, roll into a ball then flatten in palm of hand.

3 Place 1/2 teaspoon of filling in centre and remould into a smooth ball. Space around edge of large dinner plate, glaze meat balls with Worcestershire sauce.

4 Cook in microwave on high for 5 minutes. Cover with foil and stand 1 1/2 minutes.

5 Serve with a spicey plum dipping sauce.

Variations:

Dried apricots or raisins may be used instead of prunes and walnuts, and almonds in place of pine nuts. You can also make the meatballs without the stuffing, but cook 4 minutes only. Serve with tomato sauce.

Yields 16 small meat balls

lamb
and mango skewers

Photograph opposite

ingredients

1 kg/2 lb lean lamb, trimmed of visible fat and cut into 2cm/3/4in cubes

3 mangoes, cut into 2cm/3/4in cubes

24 wooden skewers

Hoisin-soy marinade

1 tablespoon finely grated fresh ginger

3/4 cup/185ml/6fl oz hoisin sauce

1/4 cup/60ml/2fl oz reduced-salt soy sauce

1/4 cup/60ml/2fl oz rice wine vinegar

1/4 cup/60ml/2fl oz vegetable oil

Method:

1 Soak skewers in cold water for at least 30 minutes before threading meat.

2 To make marinade, place ginger, hoisin and soy sauces, vinegar and oil in a bowl and mix to combine. Add lamb, toss to coat, cover and marinate in the refrigerator for at least 4 hours.

3 Thread lamb and mango cubes, alternately, onto oiled skewers. Cook on a preheated hot barbecue for 3-4 minutes each side or until tender.

Serves 8

honey-glazed
spareribs

Method:

1 To make marinade, combine chillies, garlic, spring onions, ginger, vinegar, soy sauce and honey in a non-reactive dish. Add ribs, toss to coat, cover and marinate in the refrigerator for at least 4 hours.

2 Drain ribs and reserve marinade. Cook ribs, basting occasionally with reserved marinade, on a preheated hot barbecue grill for 8-10 minutes or until ribs are tender and golden. Place on a serving platter, cover and keep warm.

3 Place remaining marinade in a saucepan, add onions, parsley, stock and lemon juice and bring to the boil. Reduce heat and simmer for 15 minutes or until sauce reduces by half. Pour mixture into a food processor or blender and process to make a purée. With motor running, pour in hot melted butter and process to combine. Serve sauce with spareribs.

Serves 8

ingredients

2 kg/4 lb pork spareribs,
trimmed of excess fat
2 onions, chopped
2 tablespoons fresh parsley, chopped
1 cup/250ml/8fl oz chicken stock
2 tablespoons lemon juice
125g/4oz butter, melted
<u>Honey-soy marinade</u>
4 small fresh red chillies, chopped
4 cloves garlic, chopped
2 spring onions, chopped
1 tablespoon fresh ginger, finely grated
1 1/2 cups/375ml/12fl oz rice-wine vinegar
1/2 cup/125ml/4fl oz reduced-salt soy
sauce
1/2 cup/170g/5 1/2oz honey

curried
trim-lamb vol-au-vents

Method:
1 *Heat non-stick pan over a high heat. Add lamb and fry for 2 minutes.*
2 *Add sauce, uncovered, for 10 minutes, stirring occasionally. Spoon into oyster cases.*
3 *Preheat oven to 180°C/350°F. Cook vol-au-vents for 10 minutes. Serve hot, garnished with sprigs of coriander (cilantro) or a herb of choice.*
Makes 24

ingredients

**200g/7oz trim-lamb eye-of-loin
or fillet, finely chopped
3/4 cup prepared satay sauce
2 x 60g/2oz packets vol-au-vents
(total 24)**

chicken
yakitori

Method:

1 *Place chicken in a glass bowl, mix in the soy sauce, honey, garlic and ginger. Cover, place in refrigerator and allow to marinate for several hours or overnight.*

2 *Thread one or two strips onto each skewer, using a weaving motion. Brush with marinade.*

3 *Heat grill or barbecue to high. Grease rack or plate with oil and arrange the skewers in a row. Cook for 2¹/₂ minutes on each side, brush with marinade as they cook. Serve immediately.*

Makes 25 small skewers

ingredients

400g/14oz chicken stir-fry
¹/₂ cup/120ml/4fl oz soy sauce
¹/₄ cup/60g/2fl oz honey
1 clove garlic, crushed
¹/₂ teaspoon ground ginger
small bamboo skewers, soaked

chicken galantine slices

Method:

1 To make filling, place chicken and sausage minces, onion, parsley, garlic, egg and black pepper to taste in a bowl and mix to combine.

2 Place each chicken breast fillet, cut side up, on a flat surface between sheets of plastic food wrap and pound lightly to make a flattened rectangle. Lay 3 slices prosciutto or ham over each rectangle. Place one-sixth of the filling lengthwise down the centre, top with a row of 5 prunes and cover with another one-sixth of the filling.

3 Wrap fillets around filling to enclose and tie at 2cm/³/₄in intervals with kitchen string. Wrap rolls in lightly buttered aluminium foil and place in a baking dish.

4 Bake for 30 minutes, remove rolls from foil and bake for 15 minutes or until chicken is cooked. Wrap rolls in clean aluminium foil and refrigerate for several hours or until cold. To serve, remove string and cut into 1cm/¹/₂in-thick slices.

Makes about 45

ingredients

3 double boneless chicken breast fillets
9 slices prosciutto or lean ham
15 pitted dessert prunes
<u>**Savoury filling**</u>
375g/12oz chicken mince
200g/6¹/₂oz sausage mince
1 onion, finely chopped
3-4 tablespoons chopped fresh parsley
2 cloves garlic, crushed
1 egg, lightly beaten
freshly ground black pepper

wellington
bread loaf

Photograph opposite

ingredients

1 Vienna loaf (soft white bread)
30g/1oz butter, melted
250g/8oz liver pâté
125g/4oz button mushrooms, sliced
750g/1 1/2 lb lean beef mince
2 tablespoons snipped fresh chives
2 teaspoons crushed black peppercorns
2 eggs, lightly beaten
1/2 beef stock cube
**1 tablespoon tomato
paste (purée)**
**<u>Red wine and
thyme sauce</u>**
30g/1oz butter
2 tablespoons flour
**1/2 cup/125ml/4fl oz
beef stock**
**1/2 cup/125ml/4fl oz dry
red wine**
freshly ground black pepper

Oven temperature 180°C, 350°F, Gas 4

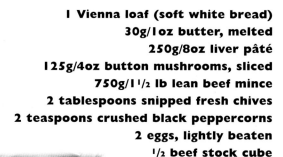

1

2

3

Method:

1 *Cut base from bread loaf and reserve. Scoop bread from centre of loaf leaving a 1cm/1/2in shell. Make bread from centre into crumbs and set aside. Brush inside of bread shell with butter, spread with pâté, then press mushroom slices into pâté.*

2 *Place 1 cup/60g/2oz reserved breadcrumbs (keep remaining breadcrumbs for another use), beef, chives, black peppercorns, eggs, stock cube and tomato paste (purée) in a bowl and mix to combine.*

3 *Spoon beef mixture into bread shell, packing down well. Reposition base and wrap loaf in aluminium foil. Place loaf on a baking tray and bake for 1 1/2 hours or until meat mixture is cooked.*

4 *To make sauce, melt butter in a saucepan over a medium heat. Stir in flour and cook,*

stirring, for 1 minute. Remove pan from heat and gradually whisk in stock and wine.
Return pan to heat and cook, stirring constantly, for 4-5 minutes or until sauce boils and thickens. Serve sauce with meatloaf.
Note: *Breadcrumbs are easy to make, simply put the bread in a food processor and process to make crumbs; if you do not have a food processor rub the bread through a sieve. It is preferable for the breadcrumbs to be made with stale bread; for this recipe either use a loaf of bread that is a day or two old or scoop out the centre of the loaf as described in the recipe, then spread the bread out on a tray and leave for 2-3 hours to become stale, before making into crumbs.*

Serves 8

ginger
pork zucchini

Method:

1 *Wash the zucchini (courgettes) and cut them into 8cm/3in pieces. With a small sharp knife. hollow out the centre by removing all the seeds, being careful not to pierce the skin.*

2 *Put the zucchini (courgette) pieces in a pot of boiling water and cook them on high heat for 3 minutes. Drain them, run them under cold water and set them aside.*

3 *In a large frypan melt the butter and sauté the onion and garlic until golden in colour. Do not brown them. Add the meat and cook the mixture over high heat for about 10 minutes or until the meat is completely cooked.*

4 *Drain on paper towels. Put the meat mixture in a food processor and add all other ingredients. Process until mixture is finely ground.*

5 *Carefully stuff the zucchini (courgettes) with the filling until firmly packed. Refrigerate them until ready to use. At serving time heat the stuffed pieces for 5-8 minutes in a 180°C/ 350°F preheated oven. Slice them and serve immediately.*

Makes 36 slices

ingredients

6 medium zucchini (courgettes)
<u>Gingered pork filling</u>
1 tablespoon butter
2 medium onions, chopped
2 cloves garlic, chopped
350g/12oz minced pork
1/2 teaspoon ground ginger
1/2 teaspoon cayenne
1 tablespoon tomato paste
1 tablespoon dry white wine
1/8 teaspoon salt dash pepper

prosciutto-
wrapped asparagus

Method:

1 Boil, steam or microwave asparagus until just tender. Drain and rinse under cold running water until cool. Drain asparagus again and dry on absorbent kitchen paper.

2 Cut each slice of prosciutto or ham lengthwise into 3 long strips and wrap each strip around an asparagus spear. Cover and refrigerate until required.

Makes about 12

ingredients

**250g/8oz fresh asparagus
spears, trimmed
4 slices prosciutto or lean ham**

beef
carpaccio

ingredients

**450g/1 lb beef fillet, sliced
into 4mm/1/8in slices
100g/3 1/2oz rocket, washed
15ml/1 tablespoon balsamic vinegar
45ml/1 1/2fl oz extra-virgin olive oil
Pecorino cheese shavings
freshly ground black pepper
salt**

Method:

1 *Lightly oil a sheet of greaseproof paper and season it lightly with salt and freshly ground black pepper.*
2 *Arrange 4 slices of beef on this (approximately 5cm apart). Place another oiled piece of greaseproof paper on top, and gently beat the meat (until the it has spread out to at least twice its former size). Repeat with the remaining meat slices.*
3 *Refrigerate until needed. Alternatively, partly freeze the meat (before slicing thinly).*
4 *Place some rocket in the centre of a plate, arrange the beef slices around the rocket, and drizzle with some balsamic vinegar and olive oil.*
5 *Serve (drizzled with balsamic vinegar and extra virgin olive oil) with shavings of Pecorino cheese and black pepper.*

Serves 6

curried
sausage puffs

Method:

1 To make filling, place mince, carrot, spring onions, chutney, curry powder and black pepper to taste in a bowl and mix to combine. Cover and refrigerate until required.

2 Roll out pastry to 3mm/¹/₈in thick and cut out a 30cm/12in square. Cut pastry square in half. Divide filling into two equal portions then shape each into a thin sausage about 30cm/12in long. Place a sausage on the long edge of each pastry rectangle and roll up. Brush edges with water to seal.

3 Cut each roll into 1cm/¹/₂in-thick slices, place on greased baking trays and bake for 12-15 minutes or until filling is cooked and pastry is golden and puffed.

Note: These savoury puffs can be prepared to the baking stage earlier in the day. Cover with plastic food wrap and store in the refrigerator until required then bake as directed in the recipe.

Makes 48

ingredients

375g/12oz prepared puff pastry
<u>Curried sausage filling</u>
375g/12oz sausage mince
1 small carrot, finely grated
2 spring onions, chopped
1 tablespoon fruit chutney
1 teaspoon curry powder
freshly ground black pepper

italian sausage
and pork roll

Photograph opposite

ingredients

500g/1 lb lean pork mince
250g/8oz Italian sausages,
casings removed
1 onion, chopped
1/2 chicken stock cube
2 slices white bread, crusts removed
2 tablespoons tomato paste (purée)
1 egg, lightly beaten
freshly ground black pepper
250g/8oz ricotta cheese, drained
2 tablespoons chopped fresh basil
4 slices pancetta or bacon, chopped
1 red capsicum (pepper),
roasted and sliced
60g/2oz pepperoni
sausage, chopped
4 black olives, sliced
4 canned anchovy
fillets, chopped
2 hard-boiled eggs,
quartered
1 tablespoon olive oil
2 tablespoons brown
sugar
1 teaspoon dried fennel seeds
1/2 teaspoon dried rosemary

Oven temperature 180°C, 350°F, Gas 4

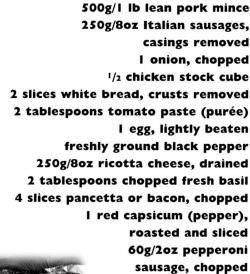

1

2

3

Method:

1 Place pork, sausage meat, onion, stock cube, bread, tomato paste (purée), egg and black pepper to taste in a food processor and process to combine. Press out meat mixture on a large piece of aluminium foil to form a 20x30cm/8x12in rectangle.

2 Spread meat with ricotta cheese and sprinkle with basil. Top with pancetta or bacon, red capsicum (pepper), pepperoni, olives, anchovies and hard-boiled eggs then roll up like a Swiss roll and wrap in foil. Place on a baking tray and bake for 40 minutes. Remove foil and drain off juices.

3 Place unwrapped roll back on baking tray and brush with oil. Combine sugar, fennel seeds and rosemary, sprinkle over roll and bake for 40 minutes longer or until cooked. **Note:** Of Italian origin, pancetta is a type of bacon available from the delicatessen section of your supermarket or Italian food shop.

Serves 6

chicken
satay

Method:

1 Combine water, peanut butter, honey, soy sauce, lemon juice, ginger and onion in a bowl. Stir in sambal oelek, if using, and mix well. Add chicken cubes, cover and marinate for at least 2 hours or overnight.

2 Soak cocktail sticks in cold water for 30 minutes, then drain. Remove chicken from marinade. Thread two pieces of chicken on each cocktail stick and set aside.

3 Pour marinade into a saucepan, bring to the boil, lower heat and simmer for about 10 minutes, or until sauce is reduced and thickened.

4 Cook chicken for about 10 minutes under a moderate grill or over hot coals, until tender. Serve four satay sticks per person, offering dipping sauce separately.

Note: You will need about 36 good-quality wooden cocktail sticks for this recipe.

Serves 8

ingredients

**500g/1 lb) chicken breast fillets, cut into 2cm/³/₄in cubes
125ml/4fl oz water
2 tablespoons smooth peanut butter
1 tablespoon honey
1 tablespoon light soy sauce
2 tablespoons lemon juice
1 teaspoon grated fresh ginger
1 onion, finely chopped
1 teaspoon sambal oelek or Tabasco sauce to taste, optional**

herb
liver pâté

Method:
1 Melt 60g/2oz of the butter in a frying pan over a low heat, add onion, garlic, thyme and rosemary and cook, stirring, for 6-8 minutes or until onion is very tender.
2 Add livers to pan, increase heat to medium and cook, stirring, until livers are brown on the outside, but still pink in the centre. Set aside to cool.
3 Place liver mixture in a food processor, add remaining butter and black pepper to taste and process until smooth. Spoon mixture into a piping bag fitted with a large star nozzle and pipe rosettes onto melba toasts or rice crackers. Arrange on a serving plate, garnish with olive slices and serve.

Makes about 30

ingredients

185g/6oz butter, softened
1 onion, chopped
2 cloves garlic, chopped
2 tablespoons fresh thyme leaves
1 tablespoon fresh rosemary leaves
750g/1 1/2 lb fresh chicken livers, cleaned
and trimmed, coarsely chopped
pinch salt
freshly ground black pepper
75g/2 1/2oz melba toasts or rice crackers
125g/4oz stuffed green olives, sliced

45

bacon-wrapped prawns (shrimp)

seafood snacks

The modern culinary trend is for light,

nutritious, easy-to-prepare meals. The remarkable properties of fish and shellfish fit these criteria well. We have a huge selection of fish available in many different forms: fresh, frozen, canned, smoked, dried and pre-prepared. The recipes that follow use a selection of these, giving you a very wide variation of taste treats.

seafood

Purchasing Seafood

The most important factor in choosing fish is freshness. Fish should not smell "fishy"; this smell is a sure sign of age or improper handling. A fresh fish has a mild odour, firm elastic flesh that springs back when pressed, clear protruding eyes, reddish or pink gills, and scales that are shiny, bright and tight to the skin.

Steaks or fillets should be fresh with a natural sheen, free from yellowing or browning around the edges. Do not buy any fish that has been frozen then defrosted for more than two days. It is always better to purchase frozen fish and defrost them at home when ready to use.

Storing Seafood
General rules to follow:

Wash both the inside and outside in cold running water. Wrap exposed flesh in plastic food wrap, which will prevent fish drying out when exposed to air. Place fish in a shallow tray-type container, ensuring not to put too much weight on bottom layer, so that fish is not squashed. Place fillets skin side up, even if skin has been removed. Keep the fish cool and moist – in ice is best – but do not allow the ice to come in direct contact with the seafood. Instead, place ice underneath and throughout the wrapped seafood.

Create continual drainage by placing the seafood on a perforated tray with a non-perforated tray beneath it to catch the melt-water. The seafood must not rest in its own fluids or melt-water because this can cause the flavour and colour to be leached out and any exposed flesh can go mushy.

Also, don't forget to label seafood with type and date.

Cooking Methods

Steaming: cooks the seafood by steam heat at temperatures greater than 100°C/210°F, retaining the subtle characteristic flavours.

If cooking over direct heat, place the prepared seafood in a single layer on a rack or in a perforated pan over the boiling liquid.

Cover tightly, but take care not to leave too long as the seafood will cook quickly.

Poaching: involves placing the seafood in just enough liquid to cover it, and gently cooking it below boiling point. The poaching liquid should be between 70°C/160°F and 80°C/175°F.

The seafood can be wrapped, placed on a rack, or put directly into the poaching liquid by bringing the liquid to a simmer and gently immersing the seafood. Bring the liquid back to poaching temperature and maintain till cooked.

Wrapping will help hold the flesh together, while a rack or perforated pan will make it easier to remove the seafood.

Boiling: involves cooking in liquid, water or stock, at 100°C/210°F.

Simmering: involves cooking in water or stock that is bubbling gently just below boiling point, between 95°C/203°F and 98°C/308°F. Simmering temperature is between poaching and boiling. There should be enough liquid to cover the seafood completely. As a general guide, it should be four times the volume of the seafood. A classic court bouillon or any other suitable stock can be used instead of salted water.

Place seafood into rapidly boiling water. Never place live crustaceans (except prawns [shrimp]) into boiling liquid as this toughens the flesh and the claws or legs may fall off. Bring the liquid back to boil, then turn the heat down to simmer and cook, covered, for the desired time.

Deep-frying: Deep-frying involves cooking food by fully immersing it in hot oil at 170°C-180°C/340°F-350°F. The temperature is important when deep-frying seafood: if too high the seafood will overcook on the outside, leaving the inside undercooked. If too low, the seafood will absorb more oil and be greasy and pale in colour.

From a health perspective, an oil with a greater proportion of monounsaturated or polyunsaturated fatty acids is recommended for deep-frying seafood.

bacon-wrapped
prawns (shrimp)

Photograph opposite

ingredients

750g/1¹/₂l lb large uncooked prawns
(shrimp), shelled and deveined,
with tails left intact
8 rashers bacon, rind removed
Herb marinade
2 tablespoons chopped fresh oregano
2 cloves garlic, crushed
¹/₂ cup/125ml/4fl oz olive oil
2 tablespoons white wine vinegar

Method:

1 To make marinade, place oregano, garlic, oil and vinegar in a bowl and whisk to combine. Add prawns (shrimp) and toss to coat. Cover and refrigerate for at least 1 hour or overnight.

2 Drain prawns (shrimp) and reserve marinade. Cut each bacon rasher into three pieces, wrap a piece of bacon around each prawn (shrimp) and secure with a wooden toothpick or cocktail stick.

3 Cook prawns (shrimp) under a preheated medium grill or on the barbecue, turning occasionally and brushing with reserved marinade, for 5 minutes or until bacon is crisp and prawns (shrimp) are cooked.

Makes about 24

prawn
(shrimp) boats

Photograph page 49

ingredients

6 stalks celery
375g/12oz medium prawns (shrimp),
cooked, shelled and deveined
1 tablespoon red lumpfish roe
1 tablespoon snipped fresh chives
Chive and caper filling
1 tablespoon snipped fresh chives
1 tablespoon chopped capers
1 tablespoon Dijon mustard
1¹/₄ cups/315g /10oz sour cream

Method:

1 To make filling, place chives, capers, mustard and sour cream in a bowl and mix to combine. Cover and refrigerate until required.

2 Trim and cut celery into 5cm/2in-long pieces. Spoon or pipe filling into celery boats. Top each boat with a prawn (shrimp) and garnish with lumpfish roe and chives.

Makes about 24

stuffed
calamari rings

Method:

1 *Pull tentacles away from head, trim. Remove membrane from tentacles and hood; wash well.*
2 *Pour boiling water over lettuce leaves, drain. Wrap tentacles in lettuce leaves, then in nori sheets. Seal with water.*
3 *Insert tentacle parcels into calamari hoods, secure with a toothpick.*
4 *Combine soy sauce, water and sugar in a saucepan and heat gently. Add calamari parcels, cover, then simmer for about 20 minutes or until tender. Remove, drain and refrigerate until cold. Serve sliced.*

Makes 36

ingredients

4 whole calamari
4 lettuce leaves
4 sheets nori (seaweed)
¹/₂ cup/120ml/4fl oz light soy sauce
¹/₂ cup/120ml/4fl oz water
2 tablespoons sugar

smoked
salmon-potato bites

Method:

1 Wash potatoes, cut in half and place cut side down. Scoop out a cavity in the top.

2 Toss in oil then bake cut side down on oven tray in moderate oven 45 minutes or until tender. Allow to cool slightly.

3 Place some salmon in each cavity, followed by a spoonful of sour cream over each. Top with a wedge of egg, then garnish with dill.

Makes 32

ingredients

16 small pontiac potatoes
¼ cup/60ml/2fl oz oil
250g/½ lb smoked salmon
½ cup/120ml/4fl oz sour cream
3 hard-boiled eggs, sliced
fresh dill for garnish

oysters
marinated with bacon

Method:
1 *In a small bowl combine soy sauce, Worcestershire sauce, and honey, set aside.*
2 *Wrap a bacon strip around each oyster, then thread two wrapped oysters on each skewer. Place skewers in a foil-lined grill pan. Pour marinade over oysters, cover and leave for 30 minutes.*
3 *Cook oysters under a preheated grill until bacon is golden. Serve immediately.*
Makes 12

ingredients

2 tablespoons soy sauce
1/2 teaspoon Worcestershire sauce
1 tablespoon honey
2 dozen oysters, shells discarded
4 rashers rindless back bacon, cut into 3cm/1 1/4in -long strips
12 small wooden skewers

54

salmon
curry puffs

Method:

1 Heat oil, add onion, chilli, garlic, coriander (cilantro), ginger, cumin and turmeric. Cook for 2 minutes.

2 Remove pan from heat and stir the lemon juice and salmon into the spice mixture. Let cool.

3 Lightly brush the first sheet of pastry with oil, then layer with a second sheet on top. Brush the second sheet with oil then layer a third sheet.

4 Cut the stack of pastry into 6 short strips. Place a spoonful of the mixture on the bottom right hand corner of each pastry strip. Fold the pastry over the filling to form a triangle, then continue folding to the end of strip, making sure to retain triangular shape.

5 Repeat with remaining pastry and filling. Place triangles on a lightly oiled oven tray, and brush the tops lightly with oil. Bake at 190°C/370°F for 12 minutes or until golden. Serve warm.

Makes 12

ingredients

1 tablespoon canola oil
1 onion, finely chopped
$^1/_2$ teaspoon each minced chilli, garlic and coriander (cilantro)
$^3/_4$ teaspoon minced ginger
$^1/_4$ teaspoon each cumin and turmeric
1 tablespoon lemon juice
210g/7$^1/_2$oz can pink salmon, drained and flaked
6 sheets filo pastry
extra tablespoon canola oil

scallops
with mango salsa

Method:

1 To make salsa, place mango, mint, lemon juice and sesame seeds in a small bowl and mix to combine. Cover and refrigerate until required.
2 Bring a large saucepan of water to the boil. Add scallops and cook for 1 minute or until tender. Using a slotted spoon remove scallops from water and place on a serving platter. Serve warm or chilled, seasoned with black pepper and topped with salsa.

Makes 16

ingredients

16 scallops in half shells
freshly ground black pepper
MANGO SALSA
1 mango, peeled and chopped
1 tablespoon chopped fresh mint
1 tablespoon lemon juice
2 tablespoons sesame seeds, toasted

seafood
pâté

Method:

1 Coarsely chop trout and prawns (shrimp) and set aside.

2 Melt butter in a saucepan over a medium heat, add spring onions and garlic and cook, stirring, for 1 minute or until onions are soft. Add trout and prawns (shrimp) and cook, stirring, until seafood is just cooked. Add brandy and cook for 1 minute, then stir in dill, cream, lemon juice and chilli sauce. Remove pan from heat and set aside to cool.

3 Transfer mixture to a food processor, season to taste with black pepper and process until smooth. Spoon mixture into a serving dish, cover and refrigerate for at least 6 hours . To serve, garnish pâté with dill sprigs and lemon slices and accompany with melba toasts.

Serves 8

ingredients

500g/1 lb trout fillets, skinned and boned
500g/1 lb uncooked prawns (shrimp), shelled and deveined
90g/3oz butter
4 spring onions, chopped
2 cloves garlic, crushed
2 tablespoons brandy
2 tablespoons chopped fresh dill
1/2 cup/125ml/4fl oz thickened cream (double)
1 tablespoon lemon juice
2 teaspoons chilli sauce
freshly ground black pepper
fresh dill sprigs and lemon slices
melba toasts or cracker biscuits

ratatouille kebabs

veggie treats

With the fruits of the fields, never

have we had it so good. Because of world-wide fast transport, we can now obtain a wide variety of fruits and vegetables all year long. When once we could only indulge in salad vegetables in summer and soup vegetables in winter, now all are available from your nearest fruit and vegetable vendor. The recipes in this chapter have been designed to take advantage of this variety and assist you in expanding your repertoire of fruit and vegetable usage.

vegetarian

Preparation Tips

Over the centuries certain combinations of herbs and foods have become traditional because they work so well together. Many of these complementary pairings are listed below. Try new combinations and make notes on your favourites.

Herbs intensify in flavour when they are dried. If substituting fresh herbs for dried, use three times the suggested amount. The exception is rosemary, which retains its natural strength when dried. Add fresh herbs to dishes at the last moment so the flavour retains its intensity. Dried herbs will need the intensity of heat to release their flavour, therefore they will need to be added earlier into the recipe.

Fruits & Vegetables

Corn: basil, chervil, chives, coriander (cilantro), marjoram, oregano, parsley, sage, tarragon, thyme.

Cruciferous vegetables (i.e. Brussels sprouts, broccoli, cauliflower, cabbage): chives, coriander (cilantro), dill, marjoram, mint, oregano, parsley, sage.

Fruits: basil, bay, chervil, chives, dill, marjoram, mint, oregano, parsley, rosemary, sage, tarragon, thyme.

Gourds (i.e. cucumber, squash, zucchini [courgettes]): chervil, chives, coriander (cilantro), dill, marjoram, mint, oregano, parsley, tarragon, thyme.

Leafy Green Vegetables (i.e. kale, silverbeet [chard], spinach): chives, dill, marjoram, oregano, parsley, thyme.

Legumes (i.e. green beans, jicama, shell beans): basil, bay, chervil, chives, cilantro, dill, marjoram, mint, oregano, parsley, rosemary, sage, tarragon, thyme.

Lettuces: basil, chervil, chives, coriander (cilantro), dill, marjoram, mint, oregano, parsley, rosemary, tarragon, thyme.

Mushrooms: basil, bay, chervil, chives, dill, marjoram, oregano, parsley, tarragon, thyme.

Onion Family (i.e. garlic, leek, onion, shallot): basil, bay, chervil, chives, coriander (cilantro), dill, marjoram, oregano, parsley, rosemary, sage, tarragon, thyme.

Root and Bulb Vegetables (i.e. beetroot, carrot, celery, fennel): chervil, chives, dill, mint, parsley, rosemary, sage, tarragon, thyme.

Tomato Family (i.e. eggplant [aubergine], capsicum [pepper], potato, tomato): basil, bay, chervil, chives, coriander (cilantro), dill, marjoram, mint, oregano, parsley, rosemary, tarragon, thyme.

Guidelines for Cooking Vegetables

The following general guidelines for cooking vegetables should be considered regardless of the cooking methods used:

- *Vegetables should be cut into uniform shapes and lengths to promote even cooking and provide an attractive finished product on your plate or table.*
- *Do not overcook. You will preserve texture, colour and nutrients if you cook vegetables for as short a time as necessary.*
- *Cook vegetables as close to serving time as possible. If held in containers they will continue to cook.*
- *When necessary, vegetables may be blanched in advance, refreshed in ice water and refrigerated. When required they may be retrieved and reheated as needed.*
- *White and red vegetables may be cooked with a small amount of acid, such as lemon or lime juice, vinegar or white wine to help retain their colour.*
- *It is important, when preparing an assortment of vegetables, to cook each type separately, then combine. Otherwise vegetables will be unevenly cooked.*
- *There is no one standard of doneness for vegetables. Each item should be evaluated on a recipe-by-recipe basis. Generally, however most vegetables are done when they are just tender when pierced with a fork or skewer.*

61

antipasto

Photograph page 61

Method:

1 Chop the cauliflower, onions, celery, zucchini (courgettes) capsicum mushrooms and tomatoes. Drain the liquid from anchovies and tuna.
2 Rinse the anchovies and tuna under hot water. Chop the anchovies and break up the tuna.
3 Combine vegetable oil, cauliflower and onions in a large pan and cook over high heat for 10 minutes, stirring frequently. Add all other ingredients except the anchovies and tuna and vinegar and cook an additional 10 minutes, stirring frequently.
4 Add the anchovies, tuna and vinegar and cook another 10 minutes, stirring frequently. Set aside to cool. Surround with mini SAOs.
5 Put the antipasto in sterilised jars and store in a refrigerator, it will keep for many weeks.

Makes enough for 20

ingredients

1 large head cauliflower
750g/26½oz sweet pickled onions
4 stalks celery
2 medium zucchini (courgettes)
3 large green capsicum (peppers)
3 large red capsicum (peppers)
800g/1¾ lb mushrooms
800g/1¾ lb plum tomatoes
112g/4oz flat anchovy fillets
350g/12½oz tin flaked tuna
250ml/9fl oz vegetable oil
750g/26½oz stuffed green olives
400g/14oz Kalamata olives
800g/1¾ lb green beans
250ml/9fl oz tomato sauce
175ml/6fl oz chilli sauce
125ml/4½fl oz white vinegar

vegetable
frittata wedges

Photograph opposite

Method:

1 Drizzle oil over the base a 23cm/9in quiche dish, then spread with onions and top with potato slices. Cover dish with aluminium foil and bake for 30 minutes or until potato is tender.
2 Arrange asparagus spears and red capsicum (pepper) and zucchini (courgette) strips like the spokes of a wheel onto top of potato, then pour over eggs and season with black pepper to taste. Scatter with Parmesan cheese.
3 Bake, uncovered, for 15 minutes or until frittata is firm. Cool for 10 minutes, then cut into thin wedges and serve.

Serves 8

ingredients

2 tablespoons vegetable oil
1 onion, very thinly sliced
1 potato, very thinly sliced
350g/11oz canned asparagus spears, drained
1 red capsicum (pepper), cut into long strips
1 zucchini (courgette), cut into long strips
6 eggs, beaten
freshly ground black pepper
2 tablespoons grated Parmesan cheese

vege
treats

dolmades

Method:

1 *Mix the onion, rice, oil, herbs, salt and two thirds lemon juice in a bowl. Boil some water and soak the vine leaves for 15 minutes, then place under cold water for 10 minutes. Lie out on a tea-towel to dry.*

2 *To wrap vine leaves: place one tablespoon of the rice mixture in the centre of the leaf and wrap like a parcel. (Use less mixture if the leaves are small.)*

3 *Place the filled leaves in a saucepan and cover with boiling water. Add the remaining lemon juice to the water. Place a plate over the top of them and cook for an hour (until the vine leaves are cooked).*

Makes approximately 35-40 dolmades

ingredients

250g/9oz onion (minced)
400g/14oz short-grain rice
150ml/5fl oz oil
1 tablespoon dill (chopped)
1/2 cup/45g/1 1/2oz mint (chopped)
1 tablespoon salt
150ml/5fl oz lemon juice
40 small vine leaves

bruschetta

Method:

1 *Grill ciabatta slices on each side for 2-3 minutes.*
2 *Brush with olive oil, spread with sun-dried tomato paste, then top with bocconcini slices and shredded basil leaves (or whole leaves).*

Serves 6

1 ciabatta loaf (cut in 1½cm/½in slices)
60ml/2fl oz olive oil
⅓ cup/80g/2½oz sun-dried tomato paste
180g/6oz bocconcini (each ball sliced into 5 slices)
½ cup/45g/1½oz basil leaves (sliced, or whole leaves)

chilli bean
corn cups

Method:

1 To make pastry, place butter and cream cheese in a food processor and process to combine. Add flour and cornmeal (polenta) and salt, then process to form a soft dough. Turn dough onto a lightly floured surface and knead until smooth. Divide dough into small balls, press into lightly greased muffins tins and bake for 20 minutes or until golden.

2 Heat oil in a frying pan over a medium heat, add onion and garlic and cook, stirring, for 5 minutes or until onion is tender. Add beef, cumin and chilli powder and stir-fry for 4-5 minutes or until is beef brown.

3 Stir in tomatoes and beans and bring to the boil. Reduce heat and simmer, stirring occasionally, for 1 hour or until most of the liquid evaporates and mixture is quite dry. Season to taste with black pepper and spoon into hot polenta cups. Serve immediately.

Makes 24

ingredients

2 tablespoons vegetable oil
1 large onion, chopped
2 cloves garlic, crushed
250g/8oz lean beef mince
2 teaspoons ground cumin
2 teaspoons chilli powder
440g/14oz canned peeled tomatoes, undrained and mashed
440g/14oz canned red kidney beans, drained and rinsed
freshly ground black pepper
<u>Polenta pastry</u>
185g/6oz butter
185g/6oz cream cheese
2 cups/250g/8oz flour
1 cup/170g/5¹/2oz cornmeal (polenta)
pinch salt

potato skins

Method:

1 *Preheat the oven to 180°C/350°F. Wash and dry each potato. Pierce with a fork and place in the preheated oven. Bake for 30 minutes or until the centre is firm but can be easily pierced with a fork.*

2 *Cool the potato, cut in quarters lengthwise and cut out the centre leaving the skin with 0.5cm/¹/₂in to 110mm/¹/₂in of potato on it.*

3 *Brush the skins with butter, then sprinkle them with salt and pepper. Bake them at 180°C/350°F for 10 minutes. Top them with chosen topping and bake for another 5-10 minutes until warmed.*

Makes 4 pieces per potato

ingredients

baking potatoes
Bacon and mushroom topping
potato pulp
sautéed bacon and mushroom
parsley
Prawn (shrimp) and chives topping
potato pulp
sour cream
chopped fresh chives
prawns (shrimp)
salt and pepper to taste
Chicken and almond Topping
potato pulp
cooked chicken
toasted pine nuts
chopped shallots
sour cream
black pepper

devilled
eggs

Method:
1 Place eggs in a saucepan, cover with cold water and bring to the boil. Stirring gently will keep the yolks centred. Discontinue stirring, reduce heat and simmer for 10 minutes. Drain eggs, then rinse under cold running water until cool enough to handle.

2 Peel eggs and cut in half lengthwise. Remove yolks and place in a bowl. Set whites aside. Add mustard, curry powder, mayonnaise and cream and mash until mixture is well combined and smooth.

3 Spoon egg yolk mixture into a piping bag fitted with a small star nozzle and pipe rosettes into reserved egg white shells. Garnish with chives or dill.

ingredients

12 eggs
1 teaspoon dry mustard
1 teaspoon curry powder
2 tablespoons mayonnaise
2 tablespoons thickened (double) cream
snipped fresh chives or dill

Makes 24

scotch
eggs

Method:

1 *Place mince, parsley and curry powder in a bowl and mix to combine. Divide mixture into four equal portions. Place each portion on a piece of plastic food wrap and press into a 12cm/5in circle.*

2 *Combine milk and egg in a shallow dish. Dip hard-boiled eggs into milk mixture then roll in flour to coat. Place an egg in the centre of each mince circle and mould around egg to enclose. Dip wrapped egg in milk mixture, then roll in breadcrumbs to coat.*

3 *Heat oil in a saucepan until a cube of bread dropped in browns in 50 seconds. Deep-fry eggs, two at a time, for 5-6 minutes or until golden. Drain on absorbent kitchen paper and cool completely. Cut in half to serve.*

Makes 8 halves

ingredients

**500g/1 lb sausage mince
2 tablespoons chopped fresh parsley
1 teaspoon curry powder
1/2 cup/60ml/2fl oz milk
1 egg, beaten
4 hard-boiled eggs, peeled
1/2 cup/60g/2oz flour
1 cup/125g/4oz dried breadcrumbs
vegetable oil for deep-frying**

guacamole

Method:

1 Cut avocados in half, remove seeds and skin. Mash roughly with a fork.
2 Plunge tomatoes into boiling water for 30 seconds, remove. Peel off skin, cut into quarters, remove and discord seeds. Cut tomatoes into small dice.
3 Combine avocado, tomato, onion, chilli, coriander (cilantro) and lemon juice. Serve with corn chips for dipping.

Serves 8

ingredients

3 avocados
2 small tomatoes
1 small onion, very finely chopped
3 red chillies, chopped
2 tablespoons fresh coriander (cilantro), chopped
2 tablespoons lemon juice
2 x 200g/6½oz packets corn chips

ratatouille
kebabs

Method:

1 *Cook onions in a saucepan of boiling water for 5 minutes. Drain, cool and cut into halves.*

2 *To make marinade, place garlic, chillies, basil, oregano, oil and wine in a bowl and mix to combine. Add onions, eggplant (aubergine), red capsicum (pepper), zucchini (courgettes), tomatoes and mushrooms, toss to coat and marinate at room temperature for at least 1 hour.*

3 *Drain vegetables and reserve marinade. Thread vegetables onto lightly oiled skewers and cook on a preheated hot barbecue grill, basting occasionally with marinade, for 4-5 minutes each side, or until cooked.*

Serves 8

ingredients

250g/8oz small pickling onions
1 small eggplant (aubergine),
cut into 2cm/³/₄in cubes
1 red capsicum (pepper), seeded and cut
into 2cm/³/₄in squares
4 zucchini (courgettes),
cut into 2cm/³/₄in pieces
250g/8oz cherry tomatoes
250g/8oz button mushrooms
<u>Herb marinade</u>
2 cloves garlic, crushed
2 small fresh red chillies, chopped
2 tablespoons chopped fresh basil
1 tablespoon chopped fresh oregano
¹/₂ cup/125ml/4fl oz olive oil
¹/₃ cup/90ml/3fl oz red wine

1

2

3

spring
roll baskets

Photograph opposite

ingredients

vegetable oil for deep-frying
8 spring roll or wonton wrappers,
each 12¹/₂cm/5in square
2 tablespoons unsalted cashews,
toasted and chopped
Pork and prawn (shrimp) filling
1 tablespoon peanut (groundnut) oil
2 teaspoons fresh ginger, finely grated
1 small fresh red chilli, finely chopped
4 spring onions, finely chopped
250g/8oz lean pork mince
125g/4oz uncooked prawns (shrimp),
shelled and deveined
1 tablespoon soy sauce
2 teaspoons fish sauce
2 teaspoons honey
2 teaspoons lemon juice
30g/1oz bean sprouts
1 small carrot, cut into thin strips
1 tablespoon fresh coriander
(cilantro), finely chopped

Method:

1 *Heat vegetable oil in a large saucepan until a cube of bread dropped in browns in 50 seconds. Place 2 spring roll or wonton wrappers, diagonally, one on top of the other, so that the corners are not matching. Shape wrappers around the base of a small ladle, lower into hot oil and cook for 3-4 minutes. During cooking keep wrappers submerged in oil by pushing down with the ladle to form a basket shape. Drain on absorbent kitchen paper. Repeat with remaining wrappers to make four baskets.*

2 *To make filling, heat peanut (groundnut) oil in a frying pan, add ginger, chilli and spring onions and stir-fry for 1 minute. Add pork and stir-fry for 5 minutes or until meat is brown.*

Add prawns (shrimp), soy sauce, fish sauce, honey, lemon juice, bean sprouts, carrot and coriander (cilantro) and stir-fry for 4-5 minutes longer or until prawns (shrimp) change colour.

3 *To serve, spoon filling into baskets and sprinkle with cashews.*
Note: *Wonton or spring roll wrappers are available frozen from Asian food shops and some supermarkets.*
Serves 4

pork and apple
cabbage rolls

Photograph opposite

ingredients

2 tablespoons vegetable oil
I onion, finely grated
2 rashers bacon, chopped
I green apple, peeled, cored and grated
I teaspoon caraway seeds
500g/I lb lean pork mince
125g/4oz brown rice, cooked
I egg, lightly beaten
freshly ground black pepper
8 large cabbage leaves
60g/2oz butter
I ¹/₂ tablespoons paprika
I ¹/₂ tablespoons flour
I tablespoon tomato paste (purée)
¹/₂ cup/125ml/4fl oz red wine
I ¹/₂ cups/375ml/12fl oz chicken stock
¹/₂ cup/125g/4oz sour cream

Method:

I *Heat oil in a frying pan over a medium heat, add onion and bacon and cook, stirring, for 3-4 minutes or until onion is soft. Stir in apple and caraway seeds and cook for 2 minutes longer. Remove pan from heat and set aside to cool.*

2 *Place pork, rice, egg, black pepper to taste and onion mixture in a bowl and mix to combine.*

3 *Boil, steam or microwave cabbage leaves until soft. Refresh under cold running water, pat dry with absorbent kitchen paper and trim stalks.*

4 *Divide meat mixture between cabbage leaves and roll up, tucking in sides. Secure with wooden toothpicks or cocktail sticks.*

5 *Melt 30g/1oz butter in a frying pan, add rolls and cook, turning several times, until lightly browned. Transfer rolls to a shallow ovenproof dish.*

6 *Melt remaining butter in pan over a medium heat, stir in paprika and flour and cook for 2 minutes. Stir in tomato paste (purée), wine and stock and bring to the boil. Reduce heat and simmer, stirring, for 5 minutes. Remove pan from heat and whisk in sour cream. Pour sauce over rolls, cover and bake for 1 hour.*

Note: *These rolls are also delicious when made using lamb mince instead of the pork. This recipe is a good way to use up leftover cooked rice and spinach or silverbeet (chard) leaves can be used instead of cabbage.*

Serves 4

tzatziki

ingredients

Method:

1 *Place cucumber, garlic, mint, parsley, yoghurt and black pepper to taste in a bowl and mix to combine. Cover and refrigerate for at least 1 hour to allow flavours to develop before serving. Serve with bread for dipping.*

Note: *Tzatziki is the fresh-tasting Greek yogurt and cucumber dip that is also delicious served with avocado salads, grilled fish or barbecued veal and lamb kebabs.*

Serves 8

**1 large cucumber, peeled, seeds removed and flesh grated
2 cloves garlic, crushed
1 tablespoon chopped fresh mint
1 tablespoon chopped fresh parsley
2¹/₂ cups/500g/1 lb natural yoghurt
freshly ground black pepper
2 French breadsticks,
torn into small pieces**

taramosalata

ingredients

Method:

1 *Peel and chop potatoes, cook in boiling water until tender, then drain and let cool.*

2 *Remove crusts from bread, combine in a bowl with 1 cup water then stand 2 minutes. Strain and press out excess water.*

3 *Place potatoes, bread, tarama, onion and pepper in a blender or processor, blend until smooth.*

4 *With blender running, gradually pour in combined olive oil and lemon juice, blend until combined.*

5 *Split pita bread in half, cut each half into wedges, and serve with taramosalata.*

Serves 8

**250g/¹/₂ lb potatoes
6 slices white bread
100g/3¹/₂oz can tarama or 60g/2oz fresh
1 onion, finely grated
freshly ground black pepper
¹/₂ cup/120ml/4fl oz olive oil
¹/₂ cup/120ml/4fl oz lemon juice
4 slices pita bread**

spicy
prawn (shrimp) dip

Method:
1 *Combine all ingredients except prawns (shrimp) in a blender or food processor. Blend well.*
2 *Stir the drained prawns (shrimp) in by hand. Chill until ready to serve. Serve with an assortment of crackers.*

**Makes about
2 ¹/₂ cups/600ml/20fl oz dip**

ingredients

**225g/8oz cream cheese
90ml/3oz mayonnaise
125ml/4¹/₂fl oz seafood cocktail sauce
1 tablespoon lemon juice
3 tablespoons spring onions, chopped
1 tablespoon parsley, chopped
120g/4¹/₂oz small prawns (shrimp)
assorted crackers**

fish
pâté

Method:
1 *Place fish fillets, shallot, lemon peel, wine and stock cube into a frypan. Simmer gently for 5 minutes or until fish is just tender.*
2 *Drain fish fillets, reserving liquid. Remove and discard any bones from fillets.*
3 *In a food processor, place boned fish, reserved liquid, butter, salt, cayenne pepper, cream and lemon juice. Purée until smooth.*
4 *Spoon into a serving bowl or individual moulds. Refrigerate for several hours.*
5 *Serve with crispbread.*

**Makes about
750g/1¹/₂ lb of pâté**

ingredients

**500g/18oz fish fillets, skinned
1 spring onions, finely chopped
2 strips lemon peel, finely chopped
125ml/4¹/₂fl oz dry white wine
1 chicken stock cube
60g/2oz butter
salt and cayenne pepper
85ml/3fl oz cream
2 teaspoons lemon juice
1 packet crispbread**

Cooking is not an exact science: one does not require finely calibrated scales, pipettes and scientific equipment to cook, yet the conversion to metric measures in some countries and its interpretations must have intimidated many a good cook.

Weights are given in the recipes only for ingredients such as meats, fish, poultry and some vegetables. Though a few grams/ounces one way or another will not affect the success of your dish.

Though recipes have been tested using the Australian Standard 250mL cup, 20mL tablespoon and 5mL teaspoon, they will work just as well with the US and Canadian 8fl oz cup, or the UK 300mL cup. We have used graduated cup measures in preference to tablespoon measures so that proportions are always the same. Where tablespoon measures have been given, these are not crucial measures, so using the smaller tablespoon of the US or UK will not affect the recipe's success. At least we all agree on the teaspoon size.

For breads, cakes and pastries, the only area which might cause concern is where eggs are used, as proportions will then vary. If working with a 250mL or 300mL cup, use large eggs (60g/2oz), adding a little more liquid to the recipe for 300mL cup measures if it seems necessary. Use the medium-sized eggs (55g/1^1/$_4$oz) with 8fl oz cup measure. A graduated set of measuring cups and spoons is recommended, the cups in particular for measuring dry ingredients. Remember to level such ingredients to ensure their accuracy.

English measures

All measurements are similar to Australian with two exceptions: the English cup measures 300mL/10fl oz, whereas the Australian cup measure 250mL/8fl oz. The English tablespoon (the Australian dessertspoon) measures 14.8mL/^{1}/$_2$fl oz against the Australian tablespoon of 20mL/^{3}/$_4$fl oz.

American measures

The American reputed pint is 16fl oz, a quart is equal to 32fl oz and the American gallon, 128fl oz. The Imperial measurement is 20fl oz to the pint, 40fl oz a quart and 160fl oz one gallon.

The American tablespoon is equal to 14.8mL/^{1}/$_2$fl oz, the teaspoon is 5mL/^{1}/$_6$fl oz. The cup measure is 250mL/8fl oz, the same as Australia.

Dry measures

All the measures are level, so when you have filled a cup or spoon, level it off with the edge of a knife. The scale below is the "cook's equivalent"; it is not an exact conversion of metric to imperial measurement. To calculate the exact metric equivalent yourself, use 2.2046 lb = 1kg or 1 lb = 0.45359kg

Metric		Imperial	
g = grams		oz = ounces	
kg = kilograms		lb = pound	
15g		^{1}/$_2$oz	
20g		^{2}/$_3$oz	
30g		1oz	
60g		2oz	
90g		3oz	
125g		4oz	^{1}/$_4$ lb
155g		5oz	
185g		6oz	
220g		7oz	
250g		8oz	^{1}/$_2$ lb
280g		9oz	
315g		10oz	
345g		11oz	
375g		12oz	^{3}/$_4$ lb
410g		13oz	
440g		14oz	
470g		15oz	
1,000g	1kg	35.2oz	2.2 lb
	1.5kg		3.3 lb

Oven temperatures

The Celsius temperatures given here are not exact; they have been rounded off and are given as a guide only. Follow the manufacturer's temperature guide, relating it to oven description given in the recipe. Remember gas ovens are hottest at the top, electric ovens at the bottom and convection-fan forced ovens are usually even throughout. We included Regulo numbers for gas cookers which may assist. To convert °C to °F multiply °C by 9 and divide by 5 then add 32.

Oven temperatures

	C°	F°	Regulo
Very slow	120	250	1
Slow	150	300	2
Moderately slow	150	325	3
Moderate	180	350	4
Moderately hot	190-200	370-400	5-6
Hot	210-220	410-440	6-7
Very hot	230	450	8
Super hot	250-290	475-500	9-10

Cake dish sizes

Metric	Imperial
15cm	6in
18cm	7in
20cm	8in
23cm	9in

Loaf dish sizes

Metric	Imperial
23x12cm	9x5in
25x8cm	10x3in
28x18cm	11x7in

Liquid measures

Metric	Imperial	Cup & Spoon
mL	fl oz	
millilitres	fluid ounce	
5mL	1/6fl oz	1 teaspoon
20mL	2/3fl oz	1 tablespoon
30mL	1fl oz	1 tablespoon plus 2 teaspoons
60mL	2fl oz	1/4 cup
85mL	2 1/2fl oz	1/3 cup
100mL	3fl oz	3/8 cup
125mL	4fl oz	1/2 cup
150mL	5fl oz	1/4 pint, 1 gill
250mL	8fl oz	1 cup
300mL	10fl oz	1/2 pint)
360mL	12fl oz	1 1/2 cups
420mL	14fl oz	1 3/4 cups
500mL	16fl oz	2 cups
600mL	20fl oz 1 pint,	2 1/2 cups
1 litre	35fl oz 1 3/4 pints,	4 cups

Cup measurements

One cup is equal to the following weights.

	Metric	Imperial
Almonds, flaked	90g	3oz
Almonds, slivered, ground	125g	4oz
Almonds, kernel	155g	5oz
Apples, dried, chopped	125g	4oz
Apricots, dried, chopped	190g	6oz
Breadcrumbs, packet	125g	4oz

	Metric	Imperial
Breadcrumbs, soft	60g	2oz
Cheese, grated	125g	4oz
Choc bits	155g	5oz
Coconut, desiccated	90g	3oz
Cornflakes	30g	1oz
Currants	155g	5oz
Flour	125g	4oz
Fruit, dried (mixed, sultanas etc)	185g	6oz
Ginger, crystallised, glace	250g	8oz
Honey, treacle, golden syrup	315g	10oz
Mixed peel	220g	7oz
Nuts, chopped	125g	4oz
Prunes, chopped	220g	7oz
Rice, cooked	155g	5oz
Rice, uncooked	220g	7oz
Rolled oats	90g	3oz
Sesame seeds	125g	4oz
Shortening (butter, margarine)	250g	8oz
Sugar, brown	155g	5oz
Sugar, granulated or caster	250g	8oz
Sugar, sifted icing	155g	5oz
Wheatgerm	60g	2oz

Length

Some of us still have trouble converting imperial length to metric. In this scale, measures have been rounded off to the easiest-to-use and most acceptable figures.

To obtain the exact metric equivalent in converting inches to centimetres, multiply inches by 2.54 whereby 1 inch equals 25.4 millimetres and 1 millimetre equals 0.03937 inches.

Metric	Imperial
mm=millimetres	in = inches
cm=centimetres	ft = feet
5mm, 0.5cm	1/4in
10mm, 1.0cm	1/2in
20mm, 2.0cm	3/4in
2.5cm	1in
5cm	2in
8cm	3in
10cm	4in
12cm	5in
15cm	6in
18cm	7in
20cm	8in
23cm	9in
25cm	10in
28cm	11in
30cm	1 ft, 12in

index